"Some years we won and sor
-Arsene Wer.

Logic Meets More Logic:

REASONS TO KEEP ARSENE WENGER

An In-Depth, And Correct, Analysis

Nasser AlNamlah

"We are young team in transition. We need the fans to be behind us. We have been unlucky with injuries. We will be stronger next year."

March 9th, 2012

-Arsene Wenger

Copyright © 2017 by Nasser AlNamlah, Justin Streight, Shannon Nakashita

All rights reserved. No part of this publication may be reproduced, distributed, or transmitted in any form or by any means, including photocopying, recording, or other electronic or mechanical methods, without the prior written permission of the publisher, except in the case of brief quotations embodied in critical reviews and certain other noncommercial uses permitted by copyright law.

Introduction:

Should Arsene Wenger's contract be extended? This question is on the mind of every true Arsenal fan, and for too many, the answer seems certain.

The Professor is under fire, shouldering the burden for Arsenal's losses with honorable stoicism. The long-time manager is no stranger to controversy, and this year is no different. This book will simplify the complicated issues surrounding Arsene Wenger and the Gunners' future with a comprehensive list of all the reasons to keep Wenger along with the most in-depth analysis possible.

Football expert Nasser AlNamlah has teamed up with editor Justin Streight and designer Shannon Nakashita to put together this guide, a must-have for any Arsenal fan. There may not have been a better case made for our manager, Arsene Wenger, ever written.

Table of Contents

WENGER'S PHILOSOPHY	1
ARSENAL'S LUCKY CHARM	15
INJURY RISK CONTROL	31
PICKING THE BEST	49
PASCAL CYGAN	51
MIKAEL SILVESTRE	53
MAROUANE CHAMAKH	57
SEBASTION SQUILLACI	61
PARK CHU-YOUNG	65
SUPER-STAR TRANSFERS	71
CHAMPION LEAGUE VICTORIES	83
VISION	93
LEGENDARY TEAM MOTIVATOR	115
NOVEMBER VICTORIES	131
PASSION	141
PERFORMANCE UNDER PRESSURE	159
WINNING MENTALITY	173
BIBLIOGRAPHY	185

Logic Meets More Logic:
REASONS TO KEEP ARSENE WENGER

Wenger's Philosophy

Logic Meets More Logic:
REASONS TO KEEP ARSENE WENGER

Logic Meets More Logic:
REASONS TO KEEP ARSENE WENGER

Logic Meets More Logic:
REASONS TO KEEP ARSENE WENGER

Logic Meets More Logic:
REASONS TO KEEP ARSENE WENGER

Logic Meets More Logic:
REASONS TO KEEP ARSENE WENGER

Logic Meets More Logic:
REASONS TO KEEP ARSENE WENGER

Logic Meets More Logic:
REASONS TO KEEP ARSENE WENGER

Logic Meets More Logic:
REASONS TO KEEP ARSENE WENGER

Logic Meets More Logic:
REASONS TO KEEP ARSENE WENGER

intentionally left blank

Logic Meets More Logic:
REASONS TO KEEP ARSENE WENGER

Logic Meets More Logic:
REASONS TO KEEP ARSENE WENGER

intentionally left blank

Logic Meets More Logic:
REASONS TO KEEP ARSENE WENGER

Logic Meets More Logic:
REASONS TO KEEP ARSENE WENGER

Logic Meets More Logic:
REASONS TO KEEP ARSENE WENGER

ARSENAL'S LUCKY CHARM

Logic Meets More Logic:
REASONS TO KEEP ARSENE WENGER

intentionally left blank

Logic Meets More Logic:
REASONS TO KEEP ARSENE WENGER

Logic Meets More Logic:
REASONS TO KEEP ARSENE WENGER

intentionally left blank

Logic Meets More Logic:
REASONS TO KEEP ARSENE WENGER

Logic Meets More Logic:
REASONS TO KEEP ARSENE WENGER

Logic Meets More Logic:
REASONS TO KEEP ARSENE WENGER

Logic Meets More Logic:
REASONS TO KEEP ARSENE WENGER

intentionally left blank

Logic Meets More Logic:
REASONS TO KEEP ARSENE WENGER

Logic Meets More Logic:
REASONS TO KEEP ARSENE WENGER

intentionally left blank

Logic Meets More Logic:
REASONS TO KEEP ARSENE WENGER

Logic Meets More Logic:
REASONS TO KEEP ARSENE WENGER

intentionally left blank

Logic Meets More Logic:
REASONS TO KEEP ARSENE WENGER

Logic Meets More Logic:
REASONS TO KEEP ARSENE WENGER

intentionally left blank

Logic Meets More Logic:
REASONS TO KEEP ARSENE WENGER

Logic Meets More Logic:
REASONS TO KEEP ARSENE WENGER

intentionally left blank

INJURY RISK CONTROL

Logic Meets More Logic:
REASONS TO KEEP ARSENE WENGER

intentionally left blank

Logic Meets More Logic:
REASONS TO KEEP ARSENE WENGER

Logic Meets More Logic:
REASONS TO KEEP ARSENE WENGER

intentionally left blank

Logic Meets More Logic:
REASONS TO KEEP ARSENE WENGER

Logic Meets More Logic:
REASONS TO KEEP ARSENE WENGER

intentionally left blank

Logic Meets More Logic:
REASONS TO KEEP ARSENE WENGER

Logic Meets More Logic:
REASONS TO KEEP ARSENE WENGER

intentionally left blank

Logic Meets More Logic:
REASONS TO KEEP ARSENE WENGER

Logic Meets More Logic:
REASONS TO KEEP ARSENE WENGER

intentionally left blank

Logic Meets More Logic:
REASONS TO KEEP ARSENE WENGER

Logic Meets More Logic:
REASONS TO KEEP ARSENE WENGER

Logic Meets More Logic:
REASONS TO KEEP ARSENE WENGER

Logic Meets More Logic:
REASONS TO KEEP ARSENE WENGER

intentionally left blank

Logic Meets More Logic:
REASONS TO KEEP ARSENE WENGER

Logic Meets More Logic:
REASONS TO KEEP ARSENE WENGER

Logic Meets More Logic:
REASONS TO KEEP ARSENE WENGER

Logic Meets More Logic:
REASONS TO KEEP ARSENE WENGER

intentionally left blank

Logic Meets More Logic:
REASONS TO KEEP ARSENE WENGER

PICKING THE BEST

Logic Meets More Logic:
REASONS TO KEEP ARSENE WENGER

Logic Meets More Logic:
REASONS TO KEEP ARSENE WENGER

PASCAL CYGAN

Logic Meets More Logic:
REASONS TO KEEP ARSENE WENGER

intentionally left blank

Logic Meets More Logic:
REASONS TO KEEP ARSENE WENGER

MIKAEL SILVESTRE

Logic Meets More Logic:
REASONS TO KEEP ARSENE WENGER

intentionally left blank

Logic Meets More Logic:
REASONS TO KEEP ARSENE WENGER

Logic Meets More Logic:
REASONS TO KEEP ARSENE WENGER

intentionally left blank

Logic Meets More Logic:
REASONS TO KEEP ARSENE WENGER

MAROUANE CAMAKH

Logic Meets More Logic:
REASONS TO KEEP ARSENE WENGER

intentionally left blank

Logic Meets More Logic:
REASONS TO KEEP ARSENE WENGER

Logic Meets More Logic:
REASONS TO KEEP ARSENE WENGER

intentionally left blank

Logic Meets More Logic:
REASONS TO KEEP ARSENE WENGER

SEBASTION SQUILLACI

Logic Meets More Logic:
REASONS TO KEEP ARSENE WENGER

intentionally left blank

Logic Meets More Logic:
REASONS TO KEEP ARSENE WENGER

Logic Meets More Logic:
REASONS TO KEEP ARSENE WENGER

intentionally left blank

Logic Meets More Logic:
REASONS TO KEEP ARSENE WENGER

PARK CHU-YOUNG

Logic Meets More Logic:
REASONS TO KEEP ARSENE WENGER

intentionally left blank

Logic Meets More Logic:
REASONS TO KEEP ARSENE WENGER

Logic Meets More Logic:
REASONS TO KEEP ARSENE WENGER

Logic Meets More Logic:
REASONS TO KEEP ARSENE WENGER

Logic Meets More Logic:
REASONS TO KEEP ARSENE WENGER

SUPER-STAR TRANSFERS

Logic Meets More Logic:
REASONS TO KEEP ARSENE WENGER

intentionally left blank

Logic Meets More Logic:
REASONS TO KEEP ARSENE WENGER

Logic Meets More Logic:
REASONS TO KEEP ARSENE WENGER

intentionally left blank

Logic Meets More Logic:
REASONS TO KEEP ARSENE WENGER

Logic Meets More Logic:
REASONS TO KEEP ARSENE WENGER

intentionally left blank

Logic Meets More Logic:
REASONS TO KEEP ARSENE WENGER

Logic Meets More Logic:
REASONS TO KEEP ARSENE WENGER

Logic Meets More Logic:
REASONS TO KEEP ARSENE WENGER

Logic Meets More Logic:
REASONS TO KEEP ARSENE WENGER

intentionally left blank

Logic Meets More Logic:
REASONS TO KEEP ARSENE WENGER

Logic Meets More Logic:
REASONS TO KEEP ARSENE WENGER

intentionally left blank

Logic Meets More Logic:
REASONS TO KEEP ARSENE WENGER

CHAMPION LEAGUE VICTORIES

Logic Meets More Logic:
REASONS TO KEEP ARSENE WENGER

intentionally left blank

Logic Meets More Logic:
REASONS TO KEEP ARSENE WENGER

Logic Meets More Logic:
REASONS TO KEEP ARSENE WENGER

intentionally left blank

Logic Meets More Logic:
REASONS TO KEEP ARSENE WENGER

Logic Meets More Logic:
REASONS TO KEEP ARSENE WENGER

intentionally left blank

Logic Meets More Logic:
REASONS TO KEEP ARSENE WENGER

Logic Meets More Logic:
REASONS TO KEEP ARSENE WENGER

intentionally left blank

Logic Meets More Logic:
REASONS TO KEEP ARSENE WENGER

Logic Meets More Logic:
REASONS TO KEEP ARSENE WENGER

intentionally left blank

Logic Meets More Logic:
REASONS TO KEEP ARSENE WENGER

Vision

Logic Meets More Logic:
REASONS TO KEEP ARSENE WENGER

intentionally left blank

Logic Meets More Logic:
REASONS TO KEEP ARSENE WENGER

Logic Meets More Logic:
REASONS TO KEEP ARSENE WENGER

intentionally left blank

Logic Meets More Logic:
REASONS TO KEEP ARSENE WENGER

Logic Meets More Logic:
REASONS TO KEEP ARSENE WENGER

intentionally left blank

Logic Meets More Logic:
REASONS TO KEEP ARSENE WENGER

Logic Meets More Logic:
REASONS TO KEEP ARSENE WENGER

intentionally left blank

Logic Meets Logic:
REASONS TO KEEP ARSENE WENGER

Logic Meets More Logic:
REASONS TO KEEP ARSENE WENGER

intentionally left blank

Logic Meets More Logic:
REASONS TO KEEP ARSENE WENGER

Logic Meets More Logic:
REASONS TO KEEP ARSENE WENGER

intentionally left blank

Logic Meets More Logic:
REASONS TO KEEP ARSENE WENGER

Logic Meets More Logic:
REASONS TO KEEP ARSENE WENGER

intentionally left blank

Logic Meets More Logic:
REASONS TO KEEP ARSENE WENGER

Logic Meets More Logic:
REASONS TO KEEP ARSENE WENGER

Logic Meets More Logic:
REASONS TO KEEP ARSENE WENGER

Logic Meets More Logic:
REASONS TO KEEP ARSENE WENGER

Logic Meets More Logic:
REASONS TO KEEP ARSENE WENGER

Logic Meets More Logic:
REASONS TO KEEP ARSENE WENGER

intentionally left blank

Logic Meets More Logic:
REASONS TO KEEP ARSENE WENGER

Logic Meets More Logic:
REASONS TO KEEP ARSENE WENGER

LEGENDARY TEAM MOTIVATOR

Logic Meets More Logic:
REASONS TO KEEP ARSENE WENGER

Logic Meets More Logic:
REASONS TO KEEP ARSENE WENGER

Logic Meets More Logic:
REASONS TO KEEP ARSENE WENGER

Logic Meets More Logic:
REASONS TO KEEP ARSENE WENGER

Logic Meets More Logic:
REASONS TO KEEP ARSENE WENGER

intentionally left blank

Logic Meets More Logic:
REASONS TO KEEP ARSENE WENGER

Logic Meets More Logic:
REASONS TO KEEP ARSENE WENGER

Logic Meets More Logic:
REASONS TO KEEP ARSENE WENGER

Logic Meets More Logic:
REASONS TO KEEP ARSENE WENGER

Logic Meets More Logic:
REASONS TO KEEP ARSENE WENGER

Logic Meets More Logic:
REASONS TO KEEP ARSENE WENGER

intentionally left blank

Logic Meets More Logic:
REASONS TO KEEP ARSENE WENGER

Logic Meets More Logic:
REASONS TO KEEP ARSENE WENGER

intentionally left blank

Logic Meets More Logic:
REASONS TO KEEP ARSENE WENGER

Logic Meets More Logic:
REASONS TO KEEP ARSENE WENGER

intentionally left blank

Logic Meets More Logic:
REASONS TO KEEP ARSENE WENGER

NOVEMBER VICTORIES

Logic Meets More Logic:
REASONS TO KEEP ARSENE WENGER

intentionally left blank

Logic Meets More Logic:
REASONS TO KEEP ARSENE WENGER

Logic Meets More Logic:
REASONS TO KEEP ARSENE WENGER

intentionally left blank

Logic Meets More Logic:
REASONS TO KEEP ARSENE WENGER

Logic Meets More Logic:
REASONS TO KEEP ARSENE WENGER

Logic Meets More Logic:
REASONS TO KEEP ARSENE WENGER

Logic Meets More Logic:
REASONS TO KEEP ARSENE WENGER

intentionally left blank

Logic Meets More Logic:
REASONS TO KEEP ARSENE WENGER

Logic Meets More Logic:
REASONS TO KEEP ARSENE WENGER

intentionally left blank

Logic Meets More Logic:
REASONS TO KEEP ARSENE WENGER

PASSION

Logic Meets More Logic:
REASONS TO KEEP ARSENE WENGER

Logic Meets More Logic:
REASONS TO KEEP ARSENE WENGER

Logic Meets More Logic:
REASONS TO KEEP ARSENE WENGER

intentionally left blank

Logic Meets More Logic:
REASONS TO KEEP ARSENE WENGER

Logic Meets More Logic:
REASONS TO KEEP ARSENE WENGER

Logic Meets More Logic:
REASONS TO KEEP ARSENE WENGER

Logic Meets More Logic:
REASONS TO KEEP ARSENE WENGER

intentionally left blank

Logic Meets More Logic:
REASONS TO KEEP ARSENE WENGER

Logic Meets More Logic:
REASONS TO KEEP ARSENE WENGER

intentionally left blank

Logic Meets More Logic:
REASONS TO KEEP ARSENE WENGER

Logic Meets More Logic:
REASONS TO KEEP ARSENE WENGER

Logic Meets More Logic:
REASONS TO KEEP ARSENE WENGER

Logic Meets More Logic:
REASONS TO KEEP ARSENE WENGER

Logic Meets More Logic:
REASONS TO KEEP ARSENE WENGER

Logic Meets More Logic:
REASONS TO KEEP ARSENE WENGER

Logic Meets More Logic:
REASONS TO KEEP ARSENE WENGER

Logic Meets More Logic:
REASONS TO KEEP ARSENE WENGER

Logic Meets More Logic:
REASONS TO KEEP ARSENE WENGER

PERFORMANCE UNDER PRESSURE

Logic Meets More Logic:
REASONS TO KEEP ARSENE WENGER

intentionally left blank

Logic Meets More Logic:
REASONS TO KEEP ARSENE WENGER

Logic Meets More Logic:
REASONS TO KEEP ARSENE WENGER

intentionally left blank

Logic Meets More Logic:
REASONS TO KEEP ARSENE WENGER

Logic Meets More Logic:
REASONS TO KEEP ARSENE WENGER

Logic Meets More Logic:
REASONS TO KEEP ARSENE WENGER

Logic Meets More Logic:
REASONS TO KEEP ARSENE WENGER

Logic Meets More Logic:
REASONS TO KEEP ARSENE WENGER

Logic Meets More Logic:
REASONS TO KEEP ARSENE WENGER

intentionally left blank

Logic Meets More Logic:
REASONS TO KEEP ARSENE WENGER

Logic Meets More Logic:
REASONS TO KEEP ARSENE WENGER

intentionally left blank

Logic Meets More Logic:
REASONS TO KEEP ARSENE WENGER

Logic Meets More Logic:
REASONS TO KEEP ARSENE WENGER

intentionally left blank

Logic Meets More Logic:
REASONS TO KEEP ARSENE WENGER

WINNING MENTALITY

Logic Meets More Logic:
REASONS TO KEEP ARSENE WENGER

intentionally left blank

Logic Meets More Logic:
REASONS TO KEEP ARSENE WENGER

Logic Meets More Logic:
REASONS TO KEEP ARSENE WENGER

Logic Meets More Logic:
REASONS TO KEEP ARSENE WENGER

Logic Meets More Logic:
REASONS TO KEEP ARSENE WENGER

intentionally left blank

Logic Meets More Logic:
REASONS TO KEEP ARSENE WENGER

Logic Meets More Logic:
REASONS TO KEEP ARSENE WENGER

intentionally left blank

Logic Meets Logic:
REASONS TO KEEP ARSENE WENGER

Logic Meets More Logic:
REASONS TO KEEP ARSENE WENGER

Logic Meets More Logic:
REASONS TO KEEP ARSENE WENGER

Logic Meets More Logic:
REASONS TO KEEP ARSENE WENGER

intentionally left blank

BIBLIOGRAPHY

Logic Meets More Logic:
REASONS TO KEEP ARSENE WENGER

intentionally left blank

Logic Meets More Logic:
REASONS TO KEEP ARSENE WENGER

Logic Meets More Logic:
REASONS TO KEEP ARSENE WENGER

Logic Meets More Logic:
REASONS TO KEEP ARSENE WENGER

Logic Meets More Logic:
REASONS TO KEEP ARSENE WENGER

intentionally left blank

Logic Meets More Logic:
REASONS TO KEEP ARSENE WENGER

First edition published by amazon.uk 2017
Printed and bound in Great Britain.
ISBN-13: 978-1544788784
ISBN-10: 1544788789

Find us on Twitter: @LogicMeetsLogic